100 Exercises for Writers

By Eileen Maki

How to Use This Book

This book has 4 sections and each section has 25 writing exercises, hence the 100 exercises for writers title (clever, huh?). However, you can get even more exercise fodder if you use each part of every exercise as a standalone prompt. If you use it that way, where each prompt, teaser, starter, and sample are separate writing prompts, you could actually get 400 exercises out of this book! In addition, if you combine 1 prompt from each of the 4 sections, you can get even more prompts. So if you took 1 random word prompt, 1 line of text prompt, 1 name prompt, and 1 setting prompt, you could use all 4 pieces in one writing piece. So you can get a lot more than 100 exercises from this book!

Each writing exercise has four parts:

Part I: The Prompt

The first part of every writing exercise is a prompt. Depending on the type of exercise, it might be a list of random words, one line of text, some character names, or a setting prompt.

Part II: The Teaser

If the prompt itself doesn't fill your mind with possibilities, the teaser is meant to get you started. I'll give you some ideas, words, phrases, or other tid-bit to get your mind working on an idea.

Part III: The Starter

If you still need a boost after the prompt and teaser, the starter will do just that, get you started. I'll give you a line or two that you can use as the beginning of your story.

Part IV: The Sample

This part will give you a sample piece that I wrote based on the prompt. This is meant to give you an idea of what you can write from the prompt.

I hope you enjoy using these exercises to get your writing started, kicked out of a rut, or pushed to completion! Remember, an exercise is not only good for the beginning of a story or poem. It can also be a great way to throw a surprise into an already started piece, get you over a writing hump when you don't know what happens next, or can help you give your ending the flourish it deserves to take your writing from ordinary to knockout power in just a few strokes of the keys (pencil, pen, or whatever you use to write!).

For each exercise, I recommend setting a timer for 10 to 15 minutes and write as much as you can in that time. Whether you write long-hand, type on a computer, or typewriter, use whatever is most comfortable for you and your writing style. Once you're done, check the Afterward section for ideas on what to do with your writing when you're finished with it.

Lose yourself in the writing, it's where I find my peace and where I hope you will find yours as well.

Happy Writing!
~ Eileen

P.S. Sign up for my free weekly
newsletter full of writing prompts,
news, and information.

To sign up for my exclusive
newsletter, go to www.EileenMaki.com
and click on the Newsletter Signup
tab.

Contents

Chapter One: Random Words 11

  Instructions 11

    Exercise # 1........................13

    Exercise # 2........................15

    Exercise # 3........................16

    Exercise # 4........................18

    Exercise # 5........................20

    Exercise # 6........................22

    Exercise # 7........................24

    Exercise # 8........................25

    Exercise # 9........................26

    Exercise # 10.......................27

    Exercise # 11.......................28

    Exercise # 12.......................29

    Exercise # 13.......................30

    Exercise # 14.......................31

    Exercise # 15.......................32

    Exercise # 16.......................33

    Exercise # 17.......................35

    Exercise # 18.......................36

    Exercise # 19.......................37

    Exercise # 20.......................39

    Exercise # 21.......................40

    Exercise # 22.......................42

    Exercise # 23.......................44

    Exercise # 24.......................45

Exercise # 25.........................46
Chapter Two: Line of Text 47
Instructions 47
Exercise # 26.........................49
Exercise # 27.........................50
Exercise # 28.........................51
Exercise # 29.........................52
Exercise # 30.........................53
Exercise # 31.........................55
Exercise # 32.........................56
Exercise # 33.........................57
Exercise # 34.........................58
Exercise # 35.........................60
Exercise # 36.........................61
Exercise # 37.........................62
Exercise # 38.........................63
Exercise # 39.........................64
Exercise # 40.........................65
Exercise # 41.........................66
Exercise # 42.........................67
Exercise # 43.........................69
Exercise # 44.........................70
Exercise # 45.........................71
Exercise # 46.........................72
Exercise # 47.........................73
Exercise # 48.........................75
Exercise # 49.........................76
Exercise # 50.........................77

Chapter Three: Characters 78

  Instructions 78

    Exercise # 51........................79

    Exercise # 52........................80

    Exercise # 53........................81

    Exercise # 54........................82

    Exercise # 55........................83

    Exercise # 56........................85

    Exercise # 57........................86

    Exercise # 58........................87

    Exercise # 59........................89

    Exercise # 60........................91

    Exercise # 61........................93

    Exercise # 62........................94

    Exercise # 63........................95

    Exercise # 64........................97

    Exercise # 65........................99

    Exercise # 66........................100

    Exercise # 67........................101

    Exercise # 68........................102

    Exercise # 69........................103

    Exercise # 70........................105

    Exercise # 71........................107

    Exercise # 72........................108

    Exercise # 73........................109

    Exercise # 74........................110

    Exercise # 75........................112

Chapter Four: Settings 114

Instructions 114
  Exercise # 76.......................115
  Exercise # 77.......................117
  Exercise # 78.......................119
  Exercise # 79.......................120
  Exercise # 80.......................121
  Exercise # 81.......................123
  Exercise # 82.......................125
  Exercise # 83.......................127
  Exercise # 84.......................129
  Exercise # 85.......................131
  Exercise # 86.......................133
  Exercise # 87.......................135
  Exercise # 88.......................137
  Exercise # 89.......................139
  Exercise # 90.......................141
  Exercise # 91.......................143
  Exercise # 92.......................145
  Exercise # 93.......................147
  Exercise # 94.......................149
  Exercise # 95.......................151
  Exercise # 96.......................153
  Exercise # 97.......................155
  Exercise # 98.......................157
  Exercise # 99.......................159
  Exercise # 100......................161
Chapter Five: Afterward.................163
 After the Exercises 163

Extra Prompts 165
  First line prompts:.................165
  Character Names:.....................165

Chapter One: Random Words

Instructions

For the Random Words exercises, you will be given a list of 3 random words. Your task is to use the words in your writing.

For example, if I give you the three words: Rose, Pen, Monkey, your task would be to include those words in your piece. Rose might make you think of your Aunt Rose or a beautiful young woman named Rose who becomes your main character. The word pen might make you think of writing or signing your name with a pen. You could make a character that is a writer, an attorney, or someone who signs a contract with a unique pen in the story or poem. For the word monkey, you could have a stuffed monkey toy, a painting of a monkey, or an actual monkey in the piece. Use your imagination and let the words paint the picture.

Random Words exercises are perhaps my favorite because they really leave the door wide open to what you can write with them. They are not restrictive. I often use random word exercises for poetry and fiction when writing.

Exercise # 1

Prompt:
Courthouse, Castle, Thermometer

Teaser:
I heard the courthouse was an old castle. It was made of marble and I bet it cost a pretty penny to keep the thermometer at a steady temperature.

Starter:
I took a deep breath and looked up at the Courthouse building. I was not prepared for this. My breath came faster and I looked down at the gym bag by my side and back at the building. I felt like a jester walking into a castle where I didn't belong. The thermometer in the lobby said 65, but I felt like it was 90 degrees in there.

Sample:
The thermometer on the front porch read 105 degrees and I felt every degree of it through my thin sun dress. It was faded and yellow, that sun dress, and flowed around me in the slight breeze. The air lifted my waist length hair and moved it lazily in the hot air like seaweed that was too heavy for the current

to move. Our house was on top of a green hill that looked out over the valley. It wasn't much, but we called it home and I loved it in the quiet space of my childhood. I imagined the whole valley was ours, not just the little plot of land that held our cottage and small farm. I imagined my daddy was the king of the valley and our modest home was a castle. He would play king of the mountain with me sometimes when he came home from the courthouse in the town below.

Exercise # 2

Prompt:
Tractor, Picket Fence, Ribbon

Teaser:
Miranda stood just inside the picket fence, watching the tractor in the field and winding her ribbon around her fingers.

Starter:
A police crime scene ribbon was strewn across the picket fence where the tractor had driven through.

Sample:
There was a huge yellow ribbon tied around the maple tree out front. David stood there, looking at the white picket fence that his father painted fresh every year. It looked pristine but David knew what it stood for. He heard the tractor coming down the road and knew his father must have seen him standing there by now.

Exercise # 3

Prompt:
Pretzel, Frog, Conversation

Teaser:
I could swear there was a frog with a pretzel trying to have a conversation with me.

Starter:
I was eating a soft pretzel with cheese and having a conversation with my friend, Milly, when a bright red frog came hopping out of the nearby trash can.

Sample:
It was warm when Mark stepped inside the store while the bell jingled merrily high above his head. His brown eyes looked past the puppy dogs and kittens and lit on what he was looking for. He jammed the rest of his pretzel in his mouth and headed for the frog aquarium. He spied the red striped frog he wanted and did a quick check to see if anyone was watching. Feeling secure, Mark reached into the tank and pulled out the little red striped frog. Putting it carefully into his jacket pocket, Mark turned and headed for the door.

With his hand on the knob, Mark heard, "Just a minute, young man. We need to have a conversation."

Exercise # 4

Prompt:
Squirrel, Mountains, Submarine

Teaser:
Visiting a squirrel in the mountains, you don't expect to find a submarine.

Starter:
It made me feel like a squirrel, running free through the mountains one moment and a squid stuck to a submarine the next.

Sample:
Hannah picked her way carefully through the blackberry bushes and peeked through the tree to the clearing. A squirrel approached her leg and she almost screamed. Clamping her mouth shut, she watched the clearing and ducked down as two figures appeared very close to her hiding spot.

"Why did we have to meet in the mountains, Tom?"

"What's the password?"

"Seriously?"

"What's the password?"

"Submarine. Can I have the phone now?"

Exercise # 5

Prompt:
Bread, Envelope, Axe

Teaser:
Alex came in the back door. He hung the axe in the mudroom and went through to the kitchen. There was a fat package on the table with a cloth wrapped around it like an envelope. He smiled. She'd made bread.

Starter:
"Give me the bread."

I handed over the envelope.

"You didn't have to give me the axe, you know."

Sample:
I knew it happened on a Wednesday because that was the day Mom normally went to the store and we'd have bread for a few days. The envelope was in the entryway when I got home from school. It was purple with black writing and I remember looking at it and wondering what was inside. I picked it up and carried it with me to the kitchen. Mom was usually in the kitchen getting

dinner prepared when I got home from school but she wasn't there that day. I checked in the axe room, well I called it the axe room because that's where Daddy kept the wood cutting axe and I wasn't supposed to go in there, but she wasn't there either.

Exercise # 6

Prompt:
Drop, Mask, Salt and Pepper Shakers

Teaser:
There was a drop of blood on the mask along with some salt and pepper shakers nearby in the alley.

Starter:
A solo rain drop slid its way down the window. I looked at the man across from me and knew I didn't ever have to wear a mask with him. I could just be myself. I scooted the salt and pepper shakers to the side of the table and reached out for his hand.

Sample:
He stood on the other side of the kitchen from me and we stared at each other. He still wore his costume and mask, but I knew it was him. I'd know him anywhere. He removed the mask and dropped it on the floor beside his feet. I felt a tear drop fall down my cheek. I stood motionless for a moment and then took a step forward. I grabbed the closest thing I could. It happened to be the salt and pepper shakers he'd given me for our first

anniversary. I held one in each hand
feeling the weight of them before I
hurled them at his head. They
shattered in an explosion of salt
and pepper. It rained down on his
head as he stood there.

"How could you?" I whispered.

Exercise # 7

Prompt:
Brain, Hammer, Swing

Teaser:
I watched him swing the hammer down and smash her skull. When he brought it up, pieces of her brain clung to the head of the hammer.

Starter:
I was sitting on the swing, thinking about Zombies wanting to eat my brain when I saw my Dad walk across the yard holding a hammer.

Sample:
In my brain I knew it was wrong but I just couldn't stop myself. I picked up the hammer, feeling the weight of it in my hand. I hefted it, testing the balance and mass of it. I looked at my target, pulled my hand back behind my shoulder. I paused, looking across the room before I released the hammer with one smooth downward swing of my arm.

Exercise # 8

Prompt:
Bucket, Fish bowl, Stethoscope

Teaser:
Putting the fish bowl on top of the bucket, I adjusted my stethoscope and prepared myself.

Starter:
The stethoscope was inside the fishbowl and I couldn't get to it from the bucket I was in.

Sample:
Putting my stethoscope in my ears, I surveyed my patient. His left hand was stuck inside a fish bowl that still contained a fish and both of his feet were wedged into a bucket that was about four inches too small for his feet. He looked up at me and grinned. He was missing a tooth in the front.

Exercise # 9

Prompt:
Camp fire, Wrench, Pencil

Teaser:
I threw the pencil into the camp fire and grabbed my wrench.

Starter:
The camp fire was warm and I was comfortable on the log with my pencil in hand. I didn't even hear Michael moving behind me with the wrench.

Sample:
The card on the table said the words 'camp fire' so I picked up my pencil and started to draw. Sitting across the table from me, Carrie sighed deeply and set her pencil down.

"What's the matter?" I asked.

"Mine looks more like a wrench than a camp fire."

Exercise # 10

Prompt:
Hat, Hot dog, Pyramids

Teaser:
I put my hat on, grabbed my hot dog, and headed out to see the pyramids.

Starter:
I followed his hat through the crowd. He stopped at the hot dog stand and headed inside the casino shaped like the Pyramids.

Sample:
Inside the pyramids, I held my lantern up high so I could see the writings on the wall. Adjusting my hat out of the light's path, I started with what looked like a dancing hot dog.

Exercise # 11

Prompt:
Scale, Horn, Horseshoe

Teaser:
Getting off the bathroom scale slowly, I heard the horn from outside signaling the start of the games. I grabbed my horseshoe case and hurried out.

Starter:
On a scale of horseshoe to horn, I was a rock.

Sample:
"A horseshoe?"

"Yes, what's wrong with that?"

"Oh nothing, it's right up there with a bathroom scale or a horn."

"I can be whatever I want for Halloween."

Exercise # 12

Prompt: Carrot, Ring, Bus

Teaser:
We boarded the bus and sat in the aisle behind a guy eating a carrot. I looked down at my ring and grinned.

Starter:
I stared at the carrot on the floor. It was half-eaten and bloody on one end. I was startled by the phone ringing and the bus honking outside for me.

Sample:
It was a ring. I didn't mean anything. Just a pretty ring with a diamond on it. I pulled the carrot out of the fridge and stared at the ring on it. I heard someone coming down the hallway so I shoved the carrot, ring and all, into my lunch bag and headed out the door. The bus was pulling up to my stop halfway down the block and I started running and waving my hands.

Exercise # 13

Prompt:
Saw, Leaf, Hourglass

Teaser:
Holding the saw in his left hand, Marie could see his hourglass tattoo. As he began sawing the limb, a single leaf floating down to land at her feet.

Starter:
Turning over the hourglass, Dr. Martin looked at me and calmly said, "Close your eyes and relax. Tell me what you see."

I closed my eyes and immediately saw something. "I see a tree. There's a saw cutting it down. A leaf falls toward me and then another. Soon there is a storm of leaves falling all around me."

Sample:
"A leaf and an hourglass?"

"I'm telling you that's what I saw."

"What the hell does that mean?"

"How should I know? I'm not the one drawing weird stuff on trees!"

Exercise # 14

Prompt:
Guitar, Funnel, Seesaw

Teaser:
There was a man on the bench nearby playing his guitar and singing softly. The seesaw went down and I felt like my guts went through a funnel.

Starter:
I didn't know how I got there. My wife was yelling at me from the kitchen about a funnel, my daughter was on the floor in front of me asking me to play my guitar again and I felt like I was on the wrong side of a seesaw.

Sample:
I sat in the grass, watching the empty playground, wondering why the seesaw went up and down with no one on it. I plucked a piece of grass and picked up my guitar. I strummed a few chords, humming to myself. The wind began to pick up and in the distance I could barely make out a funnel cloud.

Exercise # 15

Prompt:
Cheese, Airplane, Snail

Teaser:
I didn't remember boarding an airplane but I started awake to the man next to me asking if I liked cheese and the little girl across the aisle shoving her stuffed snail in my face.

Starter:
I watched the snail, leaving its trail behind as it made its way through my garden. I nibbled my piece of cheese and turned to watch an airplane pass overhead.

Sample:
I heard a crunch as I put my foot down and picked it up slowly. There was a destroyed snail on the concrete. I limped over to the grass, holding my gooey shoe off the pavement as much as possible. I began wiping my shoe in the grass, hoping the slime and guts would come off. A kid running by hit me in the arm with his toy airplane and blood began dripping down my arm. Great.

"Do you smell cheese?"

Exercise # 16

Prompt:
Soccer ball, Bomb, Movie camera

Teaser:
The bomb was the size of a soccer ball. Emily came from behind me with her movie camera, inching her way closer.

Starter:
I kicked the soccer ball away from me as I ran through the park. The food I'd eaten earlier was sitting in my stomach like a bomb about to blow. A woman with a movie camera screamed at me as I ran by.

Sample:
I knew this was a moment I would remember for the rest of my life. My dad was on the sidelines with his movie camera and I just knew he was zooming in on me. I took a deep breath and dribbled the ball down the field slowly. The opposing team watched me carefully, trying to judge my next move. I passed the ball back and forth between my feet, looking for a hole. Finally I saw it, the perfect opportunity. I faked left and then kicked the soccer ball

hard and it shot forward like a bomb toward the goal.

Exercise # 17

Prompt:
Car, High heeled shoe, Barbecue

Teaser:
A high heeled shoe stuck out of the grass, the barbecue was on its side, and the car that had crashed the party was motionless against the oak tree.

Starter:
I put my expensive high heeled shoe back in the closet and brought out my canvas flats. I could not believe we were going to a barbecue. I muttered 'white trash' under my breath as I headed to the car with a smile on my face.

Sample:
"Let's GO!" He bellowed from the doorway.

"I'm coming." I yelled back, hopping down the hallway as I tried to put my high heeled shoe on.

"It's just a barbecue for god's sake, not a ball!" Sighing, I could hear him getting in the car and slamming the door.

Exercise # 18

Prompt:
Moon, Route 95, Sewing needle

Teaser:
I plunged the sewing needle into his flesh as he drove. We were headed down Route 95 and the moon was high above us.

Starter:
Route 95 was usually clear this time of night. I pulled over by a field and got out. The moon was full and high. I grabbed my kit with the sewing needle and headed into the field.

Sample:
There was no moon to light my path. I was somewhere west of Route 95. I walked cautiously, wondering how I got a sewing needle in my hand and why I was in the middle of a forest on a Saturday night.

Exercise # 19

Prompt:
Bell, Music, Silverware

Teaser:
"I can make beautiful music with a bell or silverware!" I claimed proudly.

Starter:
I was listening to music with my headphones on when I heard the bell. I went downstairs and my Mom asked me to place the silverware on the dining table. We must be having company for dinner.

Sample:
"This silverware is dirty."

I groaned as my Mom gathered up our silverware and handed it to the waiter.

"Bell hop," She said, "can you please get us clean silverware?"

"He's not a bell hop, Mom." I said.

"Well," she tidied up her napkin and didn't look at me, "he's certainly not making any music."

"Bell hops don't..." I began and then rolled my eyes. She'd never get it.

Exercise # 20

Prompt:
Map, Microphone, Hot air balloon

Teaser:
High up in the hot air balloon, I
found a map and a microphone.

Starter:
Through the microphone, I could hear
myself breathing. I looked up as a
hot air balloon passed over in slow
motion. I looked at the map and out
at the crowd. Taking a deep breath,
I cleared my throat and began to
speak.

Sample:
"You're so full of hot air,
Michael," She screeched at me,
"You're like a... like a... one of
those, giant... hot air balloons!"

She hurled my golden microphone
award at my head. I ducked and it
hit the framed map of India on the
wall, shattering it into more pieces
than I could ever count.

Exercise # 21

Prompt:
Cupcake, Bee, Target

Teaser:
I shoved the last bite of cupcake with a candy bee on top into my mouth.

"Let's go to Target." I said, crumbs falling onto the table top.

Starter:
I waved a bee away from my cupcake and took a bite. The tops were decorated with arrows in a target and I frowned as the candy arrow crunched between my teeth.

Sample:
"We hit our target!"

My boss threw his arms wide and we all clapped and grinned at him.

"Now we need to eat a cupcake and enjoy the picnic!"

I picked up my chocolate cupcake and turned to the sound of my co-worker screaming. There was a bee between us. She waved her hand and the bee

headed in my direction. I was
frozen. I couldn't make a sound.

Exercise # 22

Prompt:
Heart, Gear, Bow and arrow

Teaser:
Grabbing my bow and arrow and other gear, I set out to find the heart of Marilyn Ziker.

Starter:
I drew a heart in the frost on the window. Next, I drew a bow and arrow, shooting the heart and breaking it into a million pieces. Sighing, I grabbed by gear and prepared to leave the diner.

Sample:
"Mom! Where's my gear?"

"How would I know? It's YOUR gear!"

"Mo-ooo-om!"

I set down my coffee and headed toward his voice. His bow and arrow was on the floor in the hallway as I headed to his room.

"Your bow and arrow are in the hall." I said.

"I know that." He rolled his eyes at me.

"Then what are you looking for?"

"The cardboard heart." He whined and I held in a laugh.

Exercise # 23

Prompt:
Anchor, Purse, Book

Teaser:
"My purse is heavy as a ship's anchor." I mumbled as I slipped my book inside and stood up.

Starter:
"An anchor? Is that how you think of me?" I grabbed my purse and stood to leave. "I'd rather be an anchor than an open book."

"That doesn't even make sense!" He growled at me.

"It does to me." I said and walked away from him.

Sample:
I stood on deck as the anchor was slowly lifted and the boat began to move. By this evening we'd be out in the open sea and I'd be on deck with a book. I smiled, didn't wave goodbye to my husband and hiked my purse over my shoulder as I headed to my room.

Exercise # 24

Prompt:
Bicycle, Mittens, Baseball

Teaser:
I shoved my hands into the mittens and hopped on my bike. I rode fast toward the baseball field.

Starter:
Strapping down the bicycle on top of the car, I pulled my mittens on and lowered my baseball cap.

Sample:
"You don't want to watch baseball with me?" He looked hurt as I pulled on my mittens.

"I told you, I am going to ride my bicycle every day, rain or shine."

"Can't you do that later?"

"No."

Exercise # 25

Prompt:
Headphones, Sword, Footprint

Teaser:
With my headphones on, I put my sword in the ready position and put my right foot on the starting footprint.

Starter:
I took my headphones off, keeping my eyes trained on the footprint on my window sill. I heard a scuffling noise and grabbed the sword from the wall.

Sample:
I pulled the sword fish out of the oven and dripped some lemon juice all over it. It looked like a juicy footprint and I chuckled as I shoved it back in and put my headphones on. This was going to be a dinner he would never forget.

Chapter Two: Line of Text

Instructions

For the Line of Text exercises, you will be given one line, a sentence or partial sentence. Your job is to set a timer for 15 minutes and write as much as you can to go along with the line you are given. The line can be the beginning of a story or book, it can be the beginning of a paragraph or chapter, or it can be whatever you want it to be.

For example, if you are given the line, 'It was a dark and stormy night...' perhaps you would think of Snoopy on top of his dog house with his typewriter. But perhaps you would think of something else. It's that something else you should explore in these exercises. Try to be unique without being too 'out there'. Unless, of course, you're writing science fiction or fantasy. Then you can be as 'out there' as you dare to be.

Have fun with these exercises! Writing should always be fun. If it ever stops being fun, you're doing something wrong.

Exercise # 26

Prompt:
When she opened the door, she wished

Teaser:
When she opened the door, she wished she would not be greeted with a surprise party.

Starter:
When she opened the door, she wished, with her eyes shut tight, that he would be there.

Sample:
When she opened the door, she wished she would see sunlight. Coming from somewhere, anywhere, that would lead her out of this underground bunker. As she entered another dark hallway with no light in sight, she began to cry.

Exercise # 27

Prompt:
He didn't understand what he'd done to her, but he would by the time she was finished.

Teaser:
He didn't understand what he'd done to her, but he would by the time she was finished. He let the letter drop to the floor and turned quickly as he heard a sound on the porch.

Starter:
He didn't understand what he'd done to her, but he would by the time she was finished. She packed her tools into the black duffel bag and loaded it into her car.

Sample:
He didn't understand what he'd done to her, but he would by the time she was finished. That's what she thought anyway, but he was ready for her. Grabbing his sniper rifle, he pulled his black mask over his face and settled in from his vantage point high in the trees to wait for her arrival.

Exercise # 28

Prompt:
The little boy's idea of heaven was

Teaser:
The little boy's idea of heaven was a playground full of empty swings and lots of dogs to play with.

Starter:
The little boy's idea of heaven was nowhere near what he would really experience.

Sample:
The little boy's idea of heaven was comforting, but Alan knew it was wrong. There was no heaven for him. He was definitely going to the other place full of heat and fire and fun.

Exercise # 29

Prompt:
The accident wasn't her fault

Teaser:
The accident wasn't her fault and he could never prove that it was.

Starter:
The accident wasn't her fault but she felt the guilt and shame as if it was.

Sample:
The accident wasn't her fault but she was not sorry it happened. Watching her brother breathe with the help of that machine was all the satisfaction she needed to know her efforts were paying off.

Exercise # 30

Prompt:
She had found something that would mean she'd never be poor again -- but there was a catch

Teaser:
She had found something that would mean she'd never be poor again -- but there was a catch. She had to sacrifice someone she loved to keep it.

Starter:
She had found something that would mean she'd never be poor again -- but there was a catch. For each million she spent, she would have to give up one of her limbs.

Sample:
She had found something that would mean she'd never be poor again -- but there was a catch. There was always a catch, wasn't there?

"What's the catch?" She asked.

"Every year you remain rich and enjoying the good life you wanted, someone you love must die."

"Someone I love? I don't love anyone."

"There are a few that you love. So if you want to remain rich, you better find some more people to love."

Exercise # 31

Prompt:
She was carried along by the crowd

Teaser:
She was carried along by the crowd.
She tried to turn around to find
him, but she couldn't.

Starter:
She was carried along by the crowd
as she screamed for them to put her
down.

Sample:
She was carried along by the crowd.
She felt her mind go numb and her
limbs succumb to the force of the
crowd and its leader. Some part of
her must remain, she reminded
herself. So she could find her
sister and escape when the time was
right.

Exercise # 32

Prompt:
He didn't want to go out on such a night, but

Teaser:
He didn't want to go out on such a night, but she would never forgive him if he didn't.

Starter:
He didn't want to go out on such a night, but he had to. They were waiting for him and they would come for him if he didn't show up.

Sample:
He didn't want to go out on such a night, but what was he going to do? Hide here until she found him? He would just have to tell her the truth. Tonight. Before it was too late for either of them to back out.

Exercise # 33

Prompt:
He was stunned -- the stranger in front of him looked exactly like the girl he'd been dreaming about

Teaser:
He was stunned -- the stranger in front of him looked exactly like the girl he'd been dreaming about. He stared at her for a few minutes before he realized she was giving him the finger.

Starter:
He was stunned -- the stranger in front of him looked exactly like the girl he'd been dreaming about. Right down to the mole on her right cheek and the flecks of brown in her left eye.

Sample:
He was stunned -- the stranger in front of him looked exactly like the girl he'd been dreaming about. He reached toward her and she took his hand.

"Come on, cowboy." She grinned. "It's time to finish that dream you've been having."

Exercise # 34

Prompt:
She decided to go to her father's grace, to ask his advice

Teaser:
She decided to go to her father's grace, to ask his advice. She dressed in the appropriate attire and covered her hair as was the custom.

Starter:
She decided to go to her father's grace, to ask his advice. She prepared herself to meet the man who she'd never known. She wondered if he would know her when he saw her.

Sample:
She decided to go to her father's grace, to ask his advice. She waited in line with the commoners for hours to see him. When she was finally presented to him, he chuckled.

"My dear, have you been waiting all this time with everyone else?"

She bowed low as was the custom of someone in her station.

"Yes, your grace."

"You do not need to wait, my child, you can come to me whenever you want."

"I did not want to take unfair advantage, your grace."

"Come here, my love, and tell me what your generous heart desires."

Exercise # 35

Prompt:
Most vivid amongst the memories of his home town

Teaser:
Most vivid amongst the memories of his home town was the water tower. Somewhere amongst all that graffiti was his name and hers.

Starter:
Most vivid amongst the memories of his home town was the run down house where he had been a happy child. They had nothing when he was young but each other and it was always enough.

Sample:
Most vivid amongst the memories of his home town was the cemetery where his brother lay at rest. He went there now, winding his way through the tombstones of so many loved ones. He knelt at Thomas' stone and saw there were fresh flowers there.

Exercise # 36

Prompt:
The first Christmas she could remember was also her best Christmas ever

Teaser:
The first Christmas she could remember was also her best Christmas ever. She had been about three, her brother five.

Starter:
The first Christmas she could remember was also her best Christmas ever. She could picture the tinsel on the tree and smell the fudge her mother would be making in the kitchen.

Sample:
The first Christmas she could remember was also her best Christmas ever. The only Christmas she wanted to remember. It was the last Christmas her mother was a part of. She disappeared the next year without a trace.

Exercise # 37

Prompt:
He had kept their mother alive in their thoughts. Too alive perhaps

Teaser:
He had kept their mother alive in their thoughts. Too alive perhaps, but that was what he had to do to get through.

Starter:
He had kept their mother alive in their thoughts. Too alive perhaps. He heard his daughter talking to her at night sometimes, like she was there.

Sample:
He had kept their mother alive in their thoughts. Too alive perhaps. She began appearing to him last year. She would always come when he called to her out of pain or loneliness. She would sit with him. Silent, always silent, but her presence soothed his soul and now he was addicted to her light.

Exercise # 38

Prompt:
They had to make sure that none of their colleagues noticed

Teaser:
They had to make sure that none of their colleagues noticed all of the missing supplies.

Starter:
They had to make sure that none of their colleagues noticed them moving a huge bag of bulky items into the trash chute. If anyone caught them, it would be the end of their freedom.

Sample:
They had to make sure that none of their colleagues noticed how close they stood to one another or how they looked at each other. If anyone suspected they were in love, they would both lose their jobs and maybe a lot more.

Exercise # 39

Prompt:
He hadn't meant to scare the child

Teaser:
He hadn't meant to scare the child.
He smiled, hoping to repair the
damage, but the small human screamed
and ran away.

Starter:
He hadn't meant to scare the child
but it couldn't be helped now. He
flashed the boy's memory and walked
away.

Sample:
He hadn't meant to scare the child
but now that he had, he might as
well make it worth his while. The
boy's eyes were huge as he walked
slowly closer. When he was right in
front of the boy, he flashed his
razor sharp teeth and the boy
screamed.

Exercise # 40

Prompt:
He didn't reply and immediately she thought: they've got him and now they're coming for me

Teaser:
He didn't reply and immediately she thought: they've got him and now they're coming for me. She went into the bedroom and began throwing clothes into a duffel bag.

Starter:
He didn't reply and immediately she thought: they've got him and now they're coming for me. She could run, but what would that get her? A lifetime of running.

Sample:
He didn't reply and immediately she thought: they've got him and now they're coming for me. Calmly she walked to her gun locker and grabbed all the rounds she had. Returning to the living room she loaded and cocked her gun, waiting for their arrival. If they wanted her too, they'd have to live long enough to get her.

Exercise # 41

Prompt:
Was it a knock that had woken her?

Teaser:
Was it a knock that had woken her?
She turned her head toward the
window, where the noise had come
from.

Starter:
Was it a knock that had woken her?
She sat up in the chair she'd fallen
asleep in and waited to hear the
noise again.

Sample:
Was it a knock that had woken her?
It came again, two quick knocks, a
pause and then one knock. She sat up
quickly. It couldn't be him. He was
dead. He was the only one who knew
the secret knock sequence. She threw
the covers from her naked legs,
grabbed her hand gun and tip toed to
the door.

Exercise # 42

Prompt:
"It's so lovely to meet you!"

It was said in a way that immediately made him feel special, the long-lost family member

Teaser:
"It's so lovely to meet you!"

It was said in a way that immediately made him feel special, the long-lost family member. But he could see the warmth did not extend to her eyes.

Starter:
"It's so lovely to meet you!"

It was said in a way that immediately made him feel special, the long-lost family member turned up at last. He greeted her with a smile and was surprised when she moved to hug him.

Sample:
"It's so lovely to meet you!"

It was said in a way that immediately made him feel special, the long-lost family member but he knew she really didn't want him there. He gave her his best fake smile and stopped her hug with an extended hand. She took it carefully as if his hand was dirty and he knew she expected him to kiss the back of her gloved hand.

Exercise # 43

Prompt:
He knew he must keep very still while he waited

Teaser:
He knew he must keep very still while he waited but he really had to pee.

Starter:
He knew he must keep very still while he waited so he metered his breath, slow in, slow out.

Sample:
He knew he must keep very still while he waited. He maneuvered into a position he could hold for hours if he needed to. Staying alert, he scanned the grounds for any movement. Seeing none, he moved his line of sight to the tops of the buildings. There he was. He could just make out the glint of a sniper rifle on top of the building closest to him.

Exercise # 44

Prompt:
To my cheating wife, I leave

Teaser:
To my cheating wife, I leave one dollar because that's all she's worth.

Starter:
To my cheating wife, I leave everything.

Sample:
To my cheating wife, I leave the house. Good luck paying for it on your new man's salary. To my loving daughter, I leave everything else with the stipulation that she can never help her mother with anything.

Exercise # 45

Prompt:
As he took in the view from the twentieth floor, the lights went out all over the city

Teaser:
As he took in the view from the twentieth floor, the lights went out all over the city and he smiled.

Starter:
As he took in the view from the twentieth floor, the lights went out all over the city. They were ready for his part of the plan now.

Sample:
As he took in the view from the twentieth floor, the lights went out all over the city and he wondered if she would come to him now. Now that no one could see her arrival. He waited on the balcony and was finally rewarded by the whoosh of her arrival. Turning, he smiled, but it wasn't her who greeted him.

Exercise # 46

Prompt:
There was something not quite right about the window

Teaser:
There was something not quite right about the window. He moved closer, reaching out his hand to touch the cool glass.

Starter:
There was something not quite right about the window. It was slightly open and the curtains fluttered in the gentle breeze.

Sample:
There was something not quite right about the window. She looked at it, trying to figure out what was wrong. She stood up, walking slowly toward the glass. She could see outside into the yard, but that too looked off somehow. Trying to open the window, she realized it was stuck shut. Starting to panic without knowing why, she went to the window next to it and it was stuck shut as well. Moving to the door, she put her hand on the knob and took a deep breath.

Exercise # 47

Prompt:
The door was closed, and as I put my hand on the handle, I felt afraid of what we might find

Teaser:
The door was closed, and as I put my hand on the handle, I felt afraid of what we might find behind it. There was a chance this could be the last door I ever opened.

Starter:
The door was closed, and as I put my hand on the handle, I felt afraid of what we might find. I looked at my partner and she nodded her readiness. I slowly turned the handle, trying to avoid any noise it might make. I heard the click of the latch releasing and then nothing.

Sample:
The door was closed, and as I put my hand on the handle, I felt afraid of what we might find on the other side. I turned the knob and threw the door open as I stepped inside, my gun at the ready and my flashlight peering into all corners of the deserted room.

"Clear!" I yelled and heard my
partner enter the room behind me.

Clay stood in the doorway, watching
my back as I checked the closet.

"There's no one here." I said,
lowering my weapon.

"That's impossible." Clay said.

Exercise # 48

Prompt:
There was a strange wailing sound coming from the next room

Teaser:
There was a strange wailing sound coming from the next room. I couldn't pinpoint why, but it didn't sound quite human.

Starter:
There was a strange wailing sound coming from the next room. I put my ear against the wall to listen. The next room was silent. Then there came a loud pounding right where my ear was and I jumped back.

Sample:
There was a strange wailing sound coming from the next room. I lay in my bed, listening to the sounds of another human being in pain and I wondered what they were in for. I had taken the blame for something someone else had done. I did it to save her and now I wish I hadn't. I heard footsteps outside my door and knew it was my turn next.

Exercise # 49

Prompt:
Bacon sandwiches always reminded her

Teaser:
Bacon sandwiches always reminded her of her mom. Candy had always loved a good bacon sandwich.

Starter:
Bacon sandwiches always reminded her of the road trip her family had taken in 1978. She was only 5 at the time, but her Momma had put some pre-cooked bacon in the cooler and they'd eaten bacon sandwiches all the way from Oregon to Texas.

Sample:
Bacon sandwiches always reminded her of breakfast with her Daddy. He would cook the bacon just right. It was nice and thick and he got it to crisp just perfectly. They would sit and eat their sandwiches together, his dripping egg yolk and hers crunching like nothing else. She smiled as she bit into the warm, salty goodness and it crunched just right.

Exercise # 50

Prompt:
They had been together for twenty-five years

Teaser:
They had been together for twenty-five years when he decided he was in love with someone else and left.

Starter:
They had been together for twenty-five years when she died of cancer in his arms. She told him to just let her die at the hospital, but he couldn't. He wanted to be there when she breathed her last.

Sample:
They had been together for twenty-five years and this was how he repaid her. She glared at him, her blue eyes closing to dangerous slits. Then she smiled, grabbed her purse and went out the front door without another word. Getting out her keys, she scraped two of them the length of his beloved pickup truck before getting into her Jeep.

Chapter Three: Characters

Instructions

For this set of exercises, you'll be given two character names, first and last. Your writing must include at least one part of each name. You can use both first names, both last names, or one first and one last. However, give yourself a high five and pat on the back if you use both first names AND both last names eloquently.

Set your timers for 15 minutes and put fingers to keys, pencil to paper, or pen to pad!

Exercise # 51

Prompt:
Dalis Cipriano, Grace Thivierge

Teaser:
Dalis Cipriano entered the main door and threw his badge down on his Sergeant's desk. Grace Thivierge looked up at him and quirked an eyebrow.

Starter:
Dalis Cipriano was a tough guy. He knew how to treat a woman, too. But that damned Grace Thivierge just refused to be wooed.

Sample:
"Hey, what's that name again?" I called to my partner across the desk from me.

"Dalis Cipriano, why?" He answered without looking up.

"I think we got a hit."

"Is Grace with him?" He looked at me now with heat in his eyes.

"I can't tell yet. Let's go"

Exercise # 52

Prompt:
Jon Balaban, Estella High

Teaser:
Jon ran when he heard the alarm. Throwing his jacket in the trash, he dashed into the street, looking for Estella.

Starter:
Estella met Jon's gaze. Her eyes were full of tears. He turned from her and walked away.

Sample:
Jon couldn't believe what he was hearing. Estella High, a spy? There was no way she was a spy. He'd known her since they were kids! He taught her how to drive and he was her first kiss. How could that tiny bundle of woman be a spy?

Exercise # 53

Prompt:
Neddy Sturm, Rhetta Geman

Teaser:
Neddy and Rhetta glanced down the hallway. The coast was clear. Giggling, hand in hand, they ran to apartment 210.

Starter:
"Neddy Sturm was his name," Rhetta said quietly, "and he was my husband."

Sample:
"Rhetta Geman!" The man at the door shouted her name, pronouncing it wrong like most people did.

She stood up and walked toward him, slinging her purse over her shoulder.

"You're Rhetta?" He asked when she stopped in front of him.

"The only Rhetta I know." She said and grinned.

Exercise # 54

Prompt:
Franciskus Cuno, Ramonda Ogden

Teaser:
Franciskus froze, his nose fighting the sneeze that was trying to blow his cover. He glanced at the woman he knew to be Ramonda Ogden. She had headphones on with her back to him.

Starter:
"Ramonda? Ramonda Ogden." Franciskus laughed a hollow laugh. "Poor kid."

Sample:
Franciskus Cuno was a dangerous man. Ramonda knew it the moment she saw him at the bar. Wiping her hands on a towel, she moved toward him.

"What can I get you?" She asked.

"Rum and Coke, please." He said and smiled.

As much as he probably meant his smile to be charming, Ramonda saw it as more of a wolf's toothy grin.

Exercise # 55

Prompt:
Derby Marubini, Janot Kimmerly

Teaser:
Derby watched the woman walk into the bar and look around. She spotted a man sitting alone at the opposite end from Derby and moved in his direction. Janot Kimmerly had no idea what Derby had in store for her.

Starter:
"Derby?! Derby Marubini, is that you?"

He winced as her shrieking voice echoed across the airport. He turned to find his high school sweetheart running toward him in impossible heels. Yep, that was Janot Kimmerly alright.

Sample:
"Janot Kimmerly." He said her name like Janet.

"Actually, it's Jan-Oh," she explained. "The t is silent."

"Right." He said. "This way."

He ushered her through a pair of white swinging doors and into a pristine white hallway. It was bright, the walls shining from the fluorescent lights overhead.

Exercise # 56

Prompt:
Ashbey Orszak, Marianna Jagers

Teaser:
"Ashbey Orszak, how could you?!"
Marianna screeched at him. "I
trusted you!"

Starter:
Marianna walked slowly, tapping on
her phone's screen as she meandered
toward her office building. She
glanced up and saw Ashbey staring at
her from across the courtyard. She
stopped walking. He had seen her,
there was no civil way out of this.

Sample:
Ashbey took Marianna's hand. He
rubbed a thumb across the back of
it. His eyes were trained on her
skin as if it was the most important
thing in the world.

"Ash?" She said softly.

He slowly raised his eyes to hers
and she was startled to see tears
swimming there.

Exercise # 57

Prompt:
Willard Losick, Giselle Berlioz

Teaser:
"Willard. Please show Giselle in."

Giselle heard her cue and stood up from the couch where she waited.

Starter:
Giselle knew she was making a terrible mistake. What else could she do? He was her brother and he needed help. She couldn't rely on their mother to help him.

Sample:
Willard stared at Giselle.

"Losick." He said. "Why?"

"I thought you were someone I used to know." She said, turning to walk away.

Exercise # 58

Prompt:
Cirilo Leslie, Saundra Osher

Teaser:
Cirilo was usually a loner, but something about Saundra Osher made him want to not be alone.

Starter:
With a name like Cirilo Leslie, people were always getting confused. Most people thought Leslie was his first name and Cirilo was his last. He had to correct people 50 percent of the time and the other 50, he just didn't care to.

Sample:
Saundra knew she was trapped. Cirilo was on the other side of the door. She could hear his ragged breathing as he leaned against the other side of the door. She could picture him pressing his ear to the door, trying to hear her. Grinning, she raised her fist to where she imagined his ear would be and banged hard three times.

Her efforts were rewarded with his loud expletives on the other side.

She laughed loud enough for him to
hear and then ran for the back door.

Exercise # 59

Prompt:
Shepard Hayes, Ira Lampros

Teaser:
Ira smacked Shepard on the back and laughed until tears came out of his eyes. Only when he stopped to wipe his eyes did he notice that Shepard wasn't laughing.

Starter:
His name was Shepard Hayes and I knew he was going to be my husband someday. The trouble was Ira Lampros. He was currently my husband and I needed to figure out a way to get rid of him.

Sample:
Ira Lampros presented his identification card and scowled at the guard.

"Where's Tom?" He barked.

"Tom is not here. My name is Shepard, Mr. Lampros."

"Well, Shepard, I expect you to learn my face and not ask me for my identification again."

Realizing Ira was the owner, Shepard swallowed.

"Yes, sir, Mr. Lampros. Just doing my job, sir."

Ira scowled harder and walked away.

Exercise # 60

Prompt:
Osmond Massam, Jayne Campedelli

Teaser:
Osmond and Jayne were destined to be together. Osmond just had to convince her.

Starter:
"Osmond Massam?" Without waiting for him to reply, she went on. "Jayne Campedelli."

The line was silent as he waited for her to continue. When she didn't, he spoke.

"Yes? What can I do for you Ms. Campedelli?"

Sample:
Jayne knew this was her last chance. She reached for Osmond's hand.

"Oz." She said his nickname softly. "Oz, you don't understand."

"What don't I understand, Jayne?" He was angry and he had every right to be.

"Oz," She could feel tears welling up in her eyes. "I'm dying, Oz."

Exercise # 61

Prompt:
Galvan Scippacercola, Jeanne
Sweeting

Teaser:
Galvan ran down the sidewalk,
pulling his gun from the holster he
ordered Jeanne to stop.

Starter:
Galvan and Jeanne knew they had
limited choices. They sat quietly,
holding hands, waiting for the
doctor to return with the results.

Sample:
"Galvan Skip... Um, Galvan?"

"I'm Galvan Scippacercola." A young
man stood up with his arm raised.

She motioned him forward and he came
to stand in front of her.

Jeanne extended her hand. "Jeanne
Sweeting."

They shook hands and Jeanne directed
him toward the corridor.

Exercise # 62

Prompt:
Kahaleel Shields, Malva Piercy

Teaser:
Kahaleel Shields knew today was
going to be a day he would always
remember. Malva Piercy walked to the
subway in a funk, having had a fight
with her sister before she left.

Starter:
Kahaleel looked at Malva's face and
wondered how anyone could love her.
Malva was classically beautiful. Her
straight nose and golden eyes
dazzled him. But he saw what was
underneath, her true self.

Sample:
Malva ran the tip of her tongue
around her lips, watching Kahaleel
the whole time. He looked very
serious, his eyes trained on her
lips. She uncrossed and crossed her
long legs under the table, running
her foot up the inside of his leg in
the process.

She picked up her drink, grinned and
took a swallow.

Exercise # 63

Prompt:
Costa Pudney, Olga Temmer

Teaser:
Costa Pudney had run with the wrong crowd all his teenage years and earned himself the kind of reputation Olga Temmer had learned to stay away from.

Starter:
Olga Temmer looked at her babies sitting on the living room floor. Picking up the phone, she stepped outside onto the patio and dialed the number she swore she would never dial.

Sample:
Costa hugged Olga close. He could feel her familiar shape molding into his, smell the sweet smell of her slightly sweaty hair.

He held her as the music started up again and began to sway.

Olga resisted at first but soon her arm came up around his neck and she settled into him.

Costa felt her letting go and his heart burst in his chest.

Exercise # 64

Prompt:
Terence High, Milka Fridlund

Teaser:
Terence knew Milka Fridlund was not someone to mess with.

Starter:
"Milka? Who names their kid Milka?"

"My parents." She said with a slightly Russian accent.

"I'm Terence." I said.

Sample:
Terence High knew it was far past time to go when Milka Fridlund fell over with a lampshade on her head.

Terence sighed and went to retrieve her from the floor. He picked her up and slung her over his shoulder. The lampshade fell to the floor and her blond hair trailed down his back.

"Goodnight everyone." Terence called over his shoulder.

Everyone laughed and called out goodbyes.

When Terence got outside, her set Milka on her feet.

"Did you get it?" He asked and she grinned.

Exercise # 65

Prompt:
Quillan Ogden, Riki Lentz

Teaser:
Quillan was aware that Riki was still staring at him but he couldn't wait any longer.

Starter:
Quillan Ogden wanted to react, but he just couldn't. His days of reacting over Riki's bad behavior were over.

Sample:
Riki watched out the window for Quillan's car. As soon as he pulled up, she kissed her dad on the cheek and went running outside. She skipped down the sidewalk and opened the passenger side of the car.

"Hi Quillan." She said as she slid into the passenger seat.

"Hey, Baby." He grinned at her and slid his eyes over her legs and back up to her breasts.

Exercise # 66

Prompt:
Felic Jag, Lolita Distaso

Teaser:
"Felic Jag."

Lolita quirked an eyebrow at her.

"Yes, that's my name. I should be on your list."

Starter:
Felic knew he was out of line but Lolita had pushed him there.

He frowned while Lolita went on and on in her annoying voice.

Sample:
Lolita Distaso was gorgeous and Italian. Her olive skin and slim hips drove Felic crazy and she knew it.

Felic crossed the room slowly, keeping her swinging hips in view as he navigated through the crowd. She caught sight of him and smiled like a cat. She turned her back to him as he moved in behind her and began to move to the music.

Exercise # 67

Prompt:
Sherd Osher, Olympie Paresky

Teaser:
Sherd wondered if Olympie was going to stand him up again.

Starter:
Sherd Osher and Olympie Paresky had been together as long as anyone could remember. They were the company's power couple. Sherd and Olympie. That's what people said. That was the couple to be like.

Sample:
Olympie was crying when she came in the front door. Sherd heard her from the kitchen and came running, wiping his hands on a dish towel.

"Olympie? What is it, Olly?" He came to her but did not touch her.

"It's Marco." She sobbed, standing still. She looked at the floor.

"What about Marco?" Dread snaked its way through Sherd's stomach.

"He's... He's..."

Exercise # 68

Prompt:
Timoteo Cecile, Adrienna
Carayannopoulos

Teaser:
"Timoteo!"

Tim heard his mother calling from
the living room. He rolled his eyes.
He'd gone by Tim since he was a
child but his mother, Adrienna,
refused to call him anything but
Timoteo.

Starter:
Timoteo Cecile was a proud man. He
would not go groveling to Adrienna
even though he knew that's what she
wanted.

Sample:
Adrienna knew she was being
followed, but she didn't mind. She
was followed by admiring men all the
time. But this time was different.
This time it was Timoteo that
followed her and she didn't mind at
all. She gave her hips a little
extra sway as she sashayed down the
sidewalk toward her apartment.

Exercise # 69

Prompt:
Parnell Perry, Juliane Ranford

Teaser:
Dr. Parnell Perry entered the exam room. Glancing at the file and then at the patient, he verified her identity automatically.

"You are Juliane Ranford?"

"Yes, Doctor."

Starter:
"Mr. Perry? Mr. Perry can you hear me?"

Nurse Juliane Ranford noted the young man's pulse and condition as they raced down the corridor to the Emergency Room.

Sample:
Juliane Ranford knew better than to trust anyone, but this man seemed different somehow. He was named after her late grandfather, after all, so he couldn't be that bad. The object of her thoughts entered the room and she stood to greet him.

"Parnell Perry?" She asked, with her hand outstretched.

"Yes. And you are Juliane Ranford?"

"Yes." She said and they both sat, avoiding making eye contact.

Exercise # 70

Prompt:
Yoshi Kagan, Prue Furth

Teaser:
"My parents were video game nerds, so they named me for their favorite character."

"Oh yeah?" Prue Furth listened while she ate her ice cream cone.

"Yeah." He waited for her to ask him what his name was. When she didn't, he offered it. "My name is Yoshi. What's yours?"

Starter:
Prue knew it was far too early in the date to feel the way she did, but she just couldn't help it. She'd fallen, and hard.

"So," Prue began, "your name is Yoshi?"

"Yes." He grimaced, waiting for her to ask the question everyone asked.

"That's an interesting name. Is it Japanese?"

He peeked over his menu to see if she was making fun of him.

Sample:
"Yoshi Kagan, you are a good man."

Yoshi looked at himself in the mirror. He had his best navy blue suit on with a white shirt and red tie.

"Yoshi Kagan, you will come out of this on top."

He grinned at himself and tightened his tie.

"As long as they haven't found Prue Furth, you're in the clear."

Exercise # 71

Prompt:
Frederique Guin, Tedi Tardif

Teaser:
Frederique smiled grimly as she
raised the hammer high over her
head. Tedi looked up at her with
pleading eyes.

Starter:
Frederique Guin was about as
interesting as her name implied. She
loved classical music and books.
Tedi Tardif was also interesting,
but in other ways. Ways Frederique
was about to find out about.

Sample:
"Frederique Guin?" Tedi said her
name like Fredrick Gwin. Frederique
rolled her eyes and stood up.

"I'm Frederique." She said. "But
please call me Freddie."

"Alright, Freddie it is." And Tedi
wrote a note beside her new
student's name in the roll book.

Exercise # 72

Prompt:
Gaspar Ratchford, Eugenio Dex

Teaser:
"My name is Gaspar." He said quietly.

"Gaspar Ratchford?" Eugenio replied.

"Yes, Gaspar Ratchford."

Eugenio's eyes got round and Gaspar laughed at his reaction.

Starter:
Gaspar and Eugenio knew they would get in big trouble if they were caught. But the thrill of their adventure was enough to outweigh the impending trouble for their actions.

Sample:
Gaspar wound the rope around his left wrist and grabbed the rope up a little higher in his right. With one foot on the large knot towards the bottom, he pushed off with his other foot and flew out over the water. The wind rushed through his short hair and he could see how far down the water was from his bird's eye view.

Exercise # 73

Prompt:
Stalewski Wallie, Medoff Mitchell

Teaser:
"Stalewski?! Your name is
Stalewski?"

"Shut up, Medoff! Like Medoff is any
better."

Starter:
Stalewski wound his way through the
masses of people, ducking under arms
and dodging around bodies. Finally
he reached the front of the crowd
and he was right in front of center
stage. His friend, Medoff, followed
close behind and was beside him
almost immediately.

Sample:
Mr. Wallie was a good teacher. He
was the kind of teacher you
remembered and thought of with fond
memories when you were much older.
But Mr. Wallie had a secret that I
would not discover until I was in my
teens. My name is Medoff Mitchell
and I was adopted.

Exercise # 74

Prompt:
Gabrielse Vivianne, Juritz Yardin

Teaser:
It was dawn and Gabrielse Vivianne lowered herself from her bedroom window to the ground with a soft thud. Juritz Yardin watched her from across the street. When Gabrielse moved silently down the street, Juritz followed.

Starter:
Ms. Vivianne was a beautiful girl with long hair the color of coal and eyes like violets. Juritz Yardin knew he would never be allowed anywhere near her, but he couldn't get her out of his head.

Sample:
Gabrielse felt something tugging on her pant leg and turned to find a small boy with huge brown eyes staring up at her. As she watched, the little boy started to cry and back away from her.

"Are you lost, little one?" She said as kindly as she could.

The little urchin shook his head up
and down and his eyes flitted around
the store.

"What is your name, child? I will
help you find your parents."

"Juritz Yardin." He said and she
knew he was one of the children who
had been left behind.

Exercise # 75

Prompt: Bret Euripides, Nikaniki Reiman

Teaser:
"Hi. This is Bret."

"Bret?"

"Yeah, Bret Euripides."

"Oh." Nikaniki said.

Starter:
Bret Euripides was an unusual name, one Nikaniki Reiman would not soon forget. Especially since he was the one she would be following for the next decade. She sighed and grabbed her bag as Bret boarded the plane.

Sample:
"Most people just call me Nikki." She said sheepishly.

"I'm Bret." He reached out his hand to take hers.

When their hands touched, Nikaniki felt a jolt up her arm and she gasped.

"Are you alright?" Bret asked and she smiled.

Chapter Four: Settings

Instructions

For the following setting prompts, write a piece using all or portions of the setting prompt. Sometimes, part of the prompt becomes a secret that is later revealed in the story. Part or all of the setting could be imaginary, not what it seems, or magical! Use your imagination and make the setting what you want it to be.

Exercise # 76

Prompt:
This large town is located in the desert and has a quaint atmosphere. It is best-known for a tumultuous history and its museum. Also, there have been many strange and unexplained disappearances over the years.

Teaser:
"What about that Collins girl or Mark Thomas' boy?"

"You can't bring them into it, they went away on purpose."

"Did they?"

Starter:
The door creaked loudly as they pushed it open and peered inside. Being the middle of the night, everything was dark and the shapes of the displays loomed above them like monsters waiting to pounce.

Sample:
"This is a large town. You should be able to find someone to go out with."

Lani sighed and rolled her eyes at her father. "Yeah, a cactus." She grumbled.

"Right, the Lannis boy. You should give him a call."

Exercise # 77

Prompt:
An unnaturally dark and shadowy grassy clearing. There is an ancient but well-preserved structure. There are no trees in sight, there is ice on the ground, and some hot springs nearby.

Teaser:
Carried stepped into the clearing and immediately felt warm. The iced over grass crunched beneath her feet and she stopped when she saw the house just inside the shadows on the other side of the clearing.

Starter:
The steam from the hot springs rose up into the dark sky like clouds being born. Drifting up and to the right, I could see the steam moving over a dark shape in the shadows. It was huge, like a castle and I had never noticed it there before.

Sample:
The meadow was beautiful and quiet. The ice on the ground crunched as I walked across the slippery surface. Moving past the hot springs to the house in the shadows, I stepped onto

the cement porch and lifted the
knocker.

Exercise # 78

Prompt:
It is cold and damp with a wide open
field. There is a shrine in the
Cypress trees surrounded by dirt and
small stones. There is a large body
of water in the distance.

Teaser:
On the horizon I could see the North
Lake winking in the sunshine. I
walked quietly yet quickly to the
Cypress clearing where dirt and
stones ringed the shrine I sought.

Starter:
Shyanne pulled her cloak tightly
around her shoulders. She had
nowhere to hide from the biting cold
in the open field as she moved north
to the Cypress grove and the shrine.

Sample:
Moving past the shrine in the
Cypress grove, Harleck traveled East
across the open field toward the
ocean on the horizon.

Exercise # 79

Prompt:
It is misty, there is a labyrinth and patches of bare ground. The labyrinth is largely covered in moss. At the center is a pond.

Teaser:
In the center of the mossy labyrinth, Sarah knew there was a pond filled with fish. She moved through the familiar twists and turns, shifting through the mist like a wraith over patches of bare ground.

Starter:
Danny wished it wasn't so damned misty in the labyrinth. He hated being here, hated feeling stupid when he couldn't find his way to the pond in the center. He didn't know how Joss did it every time.

Sample:
The labyrinth was old and covered with moss. There were patches of bare ground here and there seen through the mist and at its center rested the pond where he would seek his final peace.

Exercise # 80

Prompt:
It is windy. There is a temple and signs of ancient civilization. Spruce trees and flowers cover the ground. There is a geyser or fountain.

Teaser:
In front of the temple, an old fountain stood. It was clean and running in the midst of the trees and flowers that had grown through the cobblestone of the courtyard. It was windy here and the town surrounding the temple looked as if its inhabitants had simply dropped what they were doing and disappeared.

Starter:
The fountain gurgled to the left of where he stood. Around him were Spruce trees and flowers all over the ground. The wind gently blew the grass to whisper against his boots. Where was the temple that should be here?

Sample:
She entered the temple, her ears on point, listening for any signs of movement within the stone walls.

Hearing none, she moved away from the cheerful trees and flowers outside to the windy and shadowy depths of the temple that beckoned her.

Exercise # 81

Prompt:
The weather is tempestuous. There is a graveyard and holes in the ground. The graveyard is ancient, hung with moss and full of tall grass.

Teaser:
Moving through the tall grass, Kiera could see open graves in front of her. Spanish moss hung from the trees, draping over her face and shoulders as she moved. The dark clouds overhead swirled and coughed, threatening to let loose their water.

Starter:
Thunder clapped overhead as John Ross and Malcolm Heard worked silently. They threw shovels full of dirt over their shoulders. They were surrounded by open graves.

"If this isn't the one, John, we'll have to come back another time." Malcom said.

"I guess you're right. I just want this to be over with." John replied.

Sample:

Dark clouds swirled and tumbled above the graveyard. Long fingers of moss hung down and the tall grass reached up. There were holes in front of gravestones all over and a dark shape moved between them in silence.

Exercise # 82

Prompt:
It is frigid outside. There is a
well and a shrine. The landscape is
dead and barren with countless tiny,
sharp crystals. There is a wide,
rushing river.

Teaser:
Mikel walked to the edge of the well
and looked inside. He could not see
or smell any water and the rope was
missing a bucket. The ground between
the well and the shrine shimmered
with crystal shards. He pulled his
coat closed and zipped it as he made
his way to the nearby river.

Starter:
"What do you mean there's a river?"

"Right over here, a river."

"Yes but we're supposed to get the
water from the well."

"I don't think he'll notice the
difference."

Sample:
Ollie Frune was cold. It was snowing
and icy everywhere. Seeing the
shining spots near the well, he

moved forward only to feel a sharp
stabbing pain in the bottom of his
foot. Looking carefully he could see
what he thought was ice were really
thousands of tiny crystals all over
the ground. He could hear the river
rushing near him and took a step
back. He had found the crystal
shrine.

Exercise # 83

Prompt:
A decrepit house out in the hills. Built in 1952, it's said that an explorer who paid the house a visit never returned. Rumor has it a serial killer once lurked there.

Teaser:
Mark pushed Becca closer to the steps and laughed at her screech of terror.

"Come on, Becs." He said, "I'll protect you."

"Mark, stop it. I'm really scared."

"I know." He said.

Starter:
Tanner pedaled hard as he rode up the road to the abandoned hill house. No one ever came here so he figured he'd be safe. He didn't care about the rumors tonight. He just wanted some shelter from the cold.

Sample:
"Molly Brannon, you get back here!" Her mother screamed at her.

Her boyfriend, Tommy, hit the gas and they laughed as the car shot dirt towards her mother.

"Let's go up to the hill house." Tommy said.

"You know I don't like it there." She whined.

"I'll make you like it, baby." He smiled at her and she melted into him as he drove.

Exercise # 84

Prompt:
A fast food restaurant that focuses on overpriced, gourmet hot dogs. The tables are yellow and red with white chairs. The employees are teenagers.

Teaser:
Maria hated working at the Weenie Hut. She hated the stupid hats with wieners on them, hated the striped uniforms that made her look like a clown, and hated waiting on rude customers. She popped her gum as the next customer stepped up to the counter.

"Welcome to Weenie Hut, I'm Maria, how can I help you." She said without looking up.

"Hi, Maria." A familiar voice said.

Starter:
"I didn't say that, Ron." Mark yelled in his face.

"Yes you did. You said Paul's wiener was too small for a bun."

"I didn't mean his personal wiener!"

Ron laughed. "Personal wiener?" This made Mark start laughing too.

Sample:
The tables were yellow with red and white chairs and it looked like a nice place. Stepping up to the counter, he looked at the menu and frowned.

"All you have here is hot dogs?" He said.

"It's called Weenie Hut, sir. What did you expect?"

Nodding, he perused the menu and gave the young girl his order.

Exercise # 85

Prompt:
This old house sits on a corner lot in a small town. It is moderately sized with a large formally landscaped yard. The house is in good condition and what you can see through the windows shows pastel color schemes.

Teaser:
"I bet a witch lives there."

"What? Have you seen the inside? It's like cotton candy in there!"

"So? Maybe it's a cover!" Dan said with wide eyes.

Starter:
Tyler stood on the sidewalk in front of his new home. The large front yard and side yards were formally landscaped and pristine. The house was large and looked well cared for. Through the front windows, he could see eggshell walls and mint colored couches.

"I didn't know you Aunt Mildred, but I think I liked you." He said with a smile.

Sample:
In the small town of, Bright Swallow, on the corner of South and Main, stood a proud house on a corner lot. It had been loved and cared for over the years with a large landscaped yard and a welcoming porch. The inside was decorated in shades of pastels, soft and dreamy and comfortable.

Exercise # 86

Prompt:
Miles outside of town in a clearing surrounded by large rocks and thick trees is a grave. It is said to be the grave of an unknown prophet who fell from grace.

Teaser:
"My Dad told me it was the grave of a puppet!" Matt told the others.

"Not a puppet, you dummy!" His older brother Don said. "A prophet, like in the bible."

Starter:
They were miles outside of town when JoAnn and Maggie found themselves in a large clearing surrounded by large rocks and thick trees. They moved into the center of the clearing where some rocks were piled.

"This must be it." JoAnn said with awe.

"Now that we're here," Maggie said, "I don't think we should be doing this.

"It's the grave of a prophet." JoAnn said, "Not Christ himself!"

Sample:
In the clearing, Jonah looked around the thick trees and wondered where the others were. He could see the pile of rocks that was said to have a prophet buried underneath. He had always wondered how people could know it was a prophet but not know his name or anything about him. He heard sounds in the rocks by the trees and turned to see his friends enter the clearing.

Exercise # 87

Prompt:
You wake up in a desert with smooth brown stones outlining your body. There are shrubs and a type of grass you're not familiar with. You can hear water running nearby and the air is cool. There are a few clouds in the sky that don't look quite right.

Teaser:
Harry opened his eyes to a sky with square shaped clouds that moved as if on a conveyor belt. He realized he was laying on the ground and sat up, shaking his head. His body had been outlined with brown stones and there were shrubs and grass as far as he could see that he had never seen before.

Starter:
The sound of rushing water woke Martha and she looked around. Her body had been outlined with smooth brown stones. She rolled her eyes and stood up. She didn't recognize the shrubs and grass this time and the clouds didn't look right, so she must have miscalculated again.

Sample:
Carrie opened her eyes. She could see her husband looming over her with a concerned look on his face.

"Carrie? Oh thank GOD!" He ran his hands through his hair. "Are you alright?"

"I'm not sure." She looked around and didn't recognize anything. The shrubs were different, the grass was weird, and the clouds in the pink sky did not look right at all. "Where are we?"

"I don't know." He admitted. "But at least it's cooler here and I hear water too."

Exercise # 88

Prompt:
This large park on the outskirts of a medium sized town is always deserted. It's lovely with a pond, a gazebo, and a bandstand, but you never see anyone here. Not even birds or animals.

Teaser:
Miranda looked out from the trees at the abandoned park. The swings moved back and forth in the breeze and the trees rustled as the wind moved their leaves.

Starter:
It's not the town I would have picked had I been allowed to choose, but it would do. The house I'd purchased was big and wonderful and came at a bargain price. I knew it was because of the desolate park a few blocks away, but I wasn't going to let small town superstition keep me from a deal.

Sample:
"I dare you to stay the night there!" Matthew pointed his finger at me.

"What? Why me?" I shrieked in response.

"Because you're not afraid, or so you say."

"Who's afraid of a park, Matthew?"

"Everyone with any sense in this town is afraid of that park. You're just too stupid to be afraid, too."

"I'm not stupid. I'll prove it to you. I'll stay there tonight!"

I immediately regretted my bravado.

Exercise # 89

Prompt:
A small rectangular room that appears to be a dining/living room combo has mismatched wooden furniture. The dining chairs have ugly flowered cushions on them. The walls are red with a wallpaper border that looks like aged scroll work. The room has a warm, cozy feeling.

Teaser:
Granny had been gone for a long time before I brought myself to visit the house she'd left to me. I stood in the front room and felt her presence. I could almost see her in her favorite chair, crocheting as usual, her lips moving as she counted the stitches.

Starter:
There was no doubt it was a fixer-upper, but Mary loved it and so I would learn to love it too. The previous resident had passed away with no family, so the house was full of her old furniture and decorations. Looking at Mary's calculating look, I knew we would be shelling out some serious money to

make it look the way it did in her
beautiful head.

Sample:
It was warm and cozy in the room.
The walls were a deep red with
scroll work wallpaper borders. The
mismatched furniture somehow worked
here and added a charm I would not
have thought to add myself. The
dining chairs were covered with ugly
flowered cushions, but even those
fit with the feel of the room.

Exercise # 90

Prompt:
A coffee shop downtown that has curvaceous, abstract design elements. The shop's theme is candy and uses bright colors for their decor. Drinks are named after delicious candies.

Teaser:
Mariah stood still, perusing the drink menu. It was her turn next. She decided on the Almond Joy mocha and got her cash out. Stepping up to the counter, she looked up and froze.

Starter:
Mandy and Sarah sat at the corner table. It was colored like cotton candy and it was their favorite place to sit because it was in front of the big window and they could see everything that went on inside and outside of the coffee shop. They grinned at each other when they saw Mike Hartman walking toward the shop.

Sample:
Kila loved Thursdays. It was the day she allowed herself a treat at the coffee shop. She loved the sound of

the bell over the door as she walked in, loved the smell of ground coffee and sweetness as she made her way to the counter. Brad was behind the counter as usual. He looked so handsome in the green apron and he gave her a big, sexy smile as she stepped up to the counter.

"Snickers today, Kila?"

"How did you know?" She laughed.

"It's the third Thursday. Third Thursdays are Snickers."

Exercise # 91

Prompt:
In the town square, there is a
library, a firehouse, and a
fountain. The square is deserted. It
is the middle of the night. There is
a grassy park across the way.

Teaser:
Adam stood in the shadows of the
library, watching from his hiding
place as two figures made their way
across the park. They were hunched
over like dogs, loping along on all
fours, but Adam knew they were
human.

Starter:
Beth hurried across the park, the
dew kissed grass making her socks
wet and soggy. She ran across the
street, balancing the stack of books
she carried as she made her way to
the library. She fished her keys out
of her purse and opened the door.

Sample:
"Clint! Clint, wake up!"

Someone was shaking him pretty hard.
He popped his eyes open to see Dan
above him looking anxious.

"We've got a call, man, get up!"

Dan rushed out of the room and Clint jumped up from the sofa where he'd been dozing and ran to the ready room.

"Where is it?" Clint yelled as he put on his gear.

"12th and Main." Esther called to him from the dispatch window.

Exercise # 92

Prompt:
It's nighttime in a little seaside town. There is a huge courthouse with marble steps and a large flower garden.

Teaser:
"Fantana Malone?" Professor McGulhay called out.

Fantana grimaced. "I go by Cherry, Professor."

"Very good." He smiled and made a note in his roll book.

"Gregory Nichols?"

"I go by Apple, Professor." Greg called and the whole class erupted in laughter.

Starter:
Harold Moss was not a young man anyone wanted to mess with, including adults in the town. So when Isaac Marks saw him slinking along in the dark by the courthouse, he pretended he hadn't and kept walking. It was always a crap shoot whether seeing Harold meant he would harass or attack you or whether he

hoped you didn't see him and carried on with what he was doing. Isaac hoped it was the latter this time.

Sample:
Jolene loved the feel of the wind coming off the ocean against her face. It lifted her pale hair and she closed her eyes, enjoying the soft touch. Tears coursed down her cheeks and she didn't bother to wipe them away. Her legs dangled over the cliff as she perched at the precipice of danger. She heard someone yell behind her and turned to see flames shooting out of the courthouse and a dark figure running through the flower garden.

Exercise # 93

Prompt:
There is a river with a bridge going over it, a dentist's office is nearby. There is a large, historic bell mounted on a pedestal with a plaque.

Teaser:
Kate stood on the bridge, watching the water pass under. She was early for her dental appointment and loved the sound of the water and the cool breeze that always passed over the bridge. She knew she would be in trouble with her mother if she was late, so she reluctantly turned from the gurgling river and hurried to the dentist's office.

Starter:
Liam wasn't sure he should go in. The door stood ajar and he could hear noises coming from inside. He knocked lightly and the noise suddenly stopped but no one called out for him to come in. He heard a shuffling noise and then silence. He knocked again, louder this time.

Sample:
"And this is the bell that sounded the alarm back in 1627." The pretty

girl named Mary Ann told them as she waved her hand toward the bell. The plaque underneath repeated what she had told them.

"This way." Mary Ann instructed. She turned down a path, her dark hair flapping against her back as she pranced to the next sight.

Exercise # 94

Prompt:
It is storming and there is thunder and lightning. There is a lighthouse nearby and a hand saw on the ground in the tall grass.

Teaser:
Grabbing the hand saw, Nelson carefully crept toward the lighthouse door. Thunder cracked and almost immediately after, lightning snaked across the sky, reaching for the ground.

Starter:
Olivia ran from her car to the lighthouse door with a newspaper over her head. It was pouring outside and despite her best efforts she knew she would look like a wet cat when she finally got inside. She used her keys to open the door and stepped inside. Dropping her bags, she put the wet newspaper over the radiator to dry and removed her sopping wet coat. So much for water proofing!

Sample:
Peter stood in the top of the lighthouse watching the ocean as he brooded. Emma came up the ladder

behind him and slipped her arms around him. He touched her hands, loving the feel of her soft skin.

"You don't have to." She said quietly.

Peter sighed and moved away from her. "We've been through this, Emma."

Exercise # 95

Prompt:
There is a deer about to get into
the garden and eat all the carrots.
There is a quaint house with a
flower garden nearby.

Teaser:
"Damn it, Quincy!"

He heard her yelling his name all
the way from the back of the house.
Quincy sighed and got himself out of
his chair to go see what her problem
was. She was mumbling and working on
the fence around the vegetable
garden when he got to her.

"The deer were about to get in here
and eat all my carrots again! I told
you to fix this." She said without
even looking up at him.

Starter:
Rhonda flicked her blond hair back
over her shoulder and smiled a
flirty smile.

They were sitting on the porch of
Rhonda's small house. The fragrance
from the nearby flower garden was
strong.

"I know what I want to do." She said with a smoky voice.

"What's that?" Robert asked her, equally flirty.

"I want to rip your heart out with a spoon." She whispered and Robert smiled.

Sample:
The deer moved quietly, getting closer to the carrots every second.

Sam waited in the bushes with his shotgun.

"Come on," he whispered to himself. "Take a nibble."

The deer, as if hearing him, stood still and then bounded off into the trees.

Exercise # 96

Prompt:
A large park is in the center of town. It has outdoor chess boards and a group of people are painting a mural. There are also hot dog cart vendors nearby.

Teaser:
"Come on, Theresa! What do you have against hot dogs for crying out loud?" Tate said around his mouthful of hot dog and relish.

"Ew!" She held her mouth and pretended to dry heave. "Do you know what's in those things?"

"No."

"Exactly." She said.

Starter:
Uncle sat across from me, deliberating his next move. I rolled my eyes and looked around the park. A group of youths were painting a mural over the old graffiti that had covered the south wall of the park for decades. Sometimes I wished I did nice things like that. But then I remembered how hard it was to be nice to other people and shrugged.

Sample:
Victor moved silently, his green clothes concealing his presence in the bushes and trees on the outskirts of the park. He maneuvered around to the west side where the chess boards sat. He got as close as he could to his target and removed his pistol from his pack. Quietly attaching the silencer, he took aim and squeezed the trigger.

Exercise # 97

Prompt:
A woman is in line with a few items in her hand basket. She has an expensive purse hanging from her elbow. You overhear a few words of her conversation: Gear, Bicycle, and Helmet.

Teaser:
"Fine." She ground out and hung up her phone as she moved to the checker.

"Excuse me." I said, tapping her arm.

She turned to me with a scowl on her perfect face. "Yes?"

"If you're having trouble with a bicycle, I can recommend a good shop downtown."

She grinned a menacing grin. "If you're having trouble being an eavesdropper, I can recommend a good ear doctor."

Starter: Winnie smiled at her next customer. The woman was on the phone, talking about a bike or something. Winnie liked it when her customers were on the phone. Then she didn't have to talk to them. The woman was pretty and carried a purse that cost more than six months of Winnie's salary.

Sample:
Xavier knew it was a mistake as soon as he saw her in his line. She was on the phone talking to someone about a bicycle that was having problems with its gears. He signaled to his manager for a break but his manager shook his head and mouthed 'no'. Xavier finished with his current customer and then it was the woman's turn. She continued to speak on the phone as she shoved her basket across the counter at him. He put his head down and checked her items as quickly as he could. Realizing she had stopped talking, he chanced a look at her. She was staring at him, the person on the other end of her phone call was still talking, but she didn't respond.

"Xavier." She said and there were tears in her eyes.

Exercise # 98

Prompt:
Miniature golf course with chains along the putting area. There is a large castle as the last hole.

Teaser:
Yvonne gripped her club and squinted at the hole in the middle of the castle. This would all be over soon if she could just sink this last putt. She took a deep breath and pulled the club back. Slowly and with calculated force, she hit the little red ball and watched it move toward the hole. It veered to the right at the last moment and she closed her eyes and groaned.

"Again." Her father said behind her.

Starter:
Zack moved to step over the chain around the putting area. He felt his foot catch and saw the green turf coming closer to his face. He put his hands out in front of him and caught himself as he fell. Laughter erupted behind him and he did a few pushups, grinning. Jumping up, he looked at Laura and laughed.

"Just doing some warm ups." He claimed.

She laughed and kissed his lips lightly.

Sample:
Alexis moved to the putting area and put her ball down. Grabbing her club, she hit the ball lightly and watched it roll into the cup. She hurried to the back of the castle and watched as the ball came out and swirled around the turf before going down the last hole of the course.

"I win!" She shouted and ran to her brother. He hugged her despite his scowl.

"You always win." He grumped.

Exercise # 99

Prompt:
A zoo where elephants are studied. There is a desert display with cactus and lizards.

Teaser:
"They're so majestic." Becky said with awe.

"Just wait until you have to clean up after them. You won't think they're so majestic then, I promise." Carl replied.

Becky frowned at him and continued her observation of the lizards.

Starter:
"Why can't we just use the brushes?"

"They're too tough."

"These things have skin like used tires!" Derrick sighed and grumbled under his breath.

Dipping the sponge into the soapy water, he mounted the ladder and climbed to the top. Looking at the gray, tough skin, he applied the sponge and began scrubbing.

Sample:

Erica stood at the fence, looking at the smaller elephant. She assumed it was younger than the others, but not a baby. He saw her standing there and moved to stand in front of her. He turned his head and she met his gaze with one of her own. She tried to convey love and dedication with her eyes. Flick snorted and waved his trunk around before raising it over the fence to touch her head.

Exercise # 100

Prompt:
A farmer's market where a farmer is
loading produce from his trailer
behind his tractor into baskets.

Teaser:
Gabbie grabbed a few more baskets
and put them on the table. Fruit was
always more popular at these things
than vegetables, but she had brought
some of each just in case.

She glanced around at her fellow
farmers and smiled. Even though she
didn't make much money, she made
enough to live off of and she loved
farming. She was finally happy.

Starter:
Hank approached from her left side
and began unloading vegetables and
putting them into the waiting
baskets.

"What do you think you're doing?"
Ilene ground out through clenched
teeth.

"I said I would help and so I am."
He said as he worked.

"That was before."

Sample:
Jack knew this was going to be a rough day for sales. The sky was gray and dark clouds were rolling slowly overhead. He unloaded his produce and put them into cute baskets with ribbon on them. That had been Karen's idea. To make the baskets prettier than just plain green plastic. He smiled as he remembered her cutting each piece of ribbon the same length and tying them to the baskets before she curled it with a pair of scissors.

Chapter Five: Afterward

After the Exercises

Ok, so you've written some great stuff. Now what? What should you do with it now? Well, depending on what you want to do with the polished product, you might want to do different things with your finished writing piece.

However, no matter what you intend to do with it, you always want to edit your writing after it's finished. The best thing to do is to set the writing aside for a while before you attempt to edit it. The optimal length of time is at least 48 hours or 2 days. This gives your mind an opportunity to think about other things and when you come back to edit your writing, you will have a fresh perspective and catch things you might not catch otherwise.

Once you have edited your work, you can do many things with it. Here are just a few I can recommend:

- Use several pieces for a short story collection.
- Write a longer piece and submit it to short story contests.
- Submit your work to magazines and other venues for publication.

Writing is so fun and really gets your creative juices flowing. The most important thing, even if your goal is not publication, is to be creative, let your mind run away with itself and write something even you did not expect.

Extra Prompts

First line prompts:

* She couldn't believe it. Was it really him?

* She took a deep breath and said to her boss --

* She had followed the woman for days and at last her patience was paying off

* She suddenly realized she might be alone for the rest of her life

* She had missed the last train and there was only one person she

Character Names:

* Jock Fellows, Kali Nicklas

* Daren Truss, Janene Bunk

* Rolando Lai, Sindee Jalisi

* Estevan Mahdi, April Yashar

* Archambalut Shakis, Brooke Scales

* Graham Mallon, Catina Bassow